TANDEM

There Was a Fair M

More of the hilarious and ribald adventures of the young ladies, students, jolly old Bishops and sailors who appeared in Hugh De Witt's previous book of limericks.

This is an unashamedly gay collection of vintage bawdry, some old, some new, many unpublished—something for everyone. Did you know the one about the Fair Maid of . . . ? Have a look and see what you've missed!

There Was a Fair Maid

Hugh De Witt

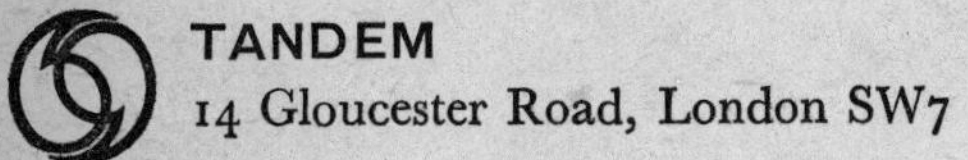

TANDEM
14 Gloucester Road, London SW7

First published in Great Britain by
Universal-Tandem Publishing Co. Ltd. 1969

Made and printed in Great Britain by
The Garden City Press Ltd., Letchworth, Herts.

PREFACE

In response to public demand, as they say, here is a second anthology of limericks. The best-selling success of *There Was a Young Lady* has shown that enthusiasm for the traditional limerick remains as strong as ever it was, and among all classes at that. Students of sexual and social attitudes can make of this what they may: but they will have a difficult task.

For the limerick has a way of eluding all attempts at analysis and of confounding all theories. Its unflagging popularity must puzzle those who argue that the only reason for its existence is to cock a snook at certain stiff-faced attitudes towards the body's natural functions and plumbing equipment. One suspects, of course, that permissiveness may not be as widespread as is claimed in British society; there is more to Britain, after all, than certain "with-it" districts of London. But the limerick, with its zany note of fantasy, not only mocks prudish and puritanical attitudes towards the body—it manages to mock itself.

Of only one thing can we be certain: the limerick is alive and well and lustily swinging in Britain today, the most virile of centenarians. We can each nurture our theories as to why. Its well-turned form and lively rhythm must be an important factor; probably more important than content. As the versifier said:

Well, it's mostly the shape of the thing
That gives the old limerick wing:
  Those accordian pleats
  Full of airy conceits
Take it up like a kite on a string.

HUGH DE WITT

1

There was a fair maid with such graces
That her curves cried aloud for embraces.
  "You look," cried each he,
  "Like a million to me—
Invested in all the right places."

2

There was a young lady named Cleo,
Who desired a violinist from Rio.
  As she took down her panties,
  She said: "Please, no *andantes*!
I want this done *allegro con brio*!"

3

There was a young man from Antigua,
Who said to his girl: "What a prig you are!
  Whenever we lay
  You refuse to display
The nethermost part of your figua."

4

It always delights me at Hanks
To walk up the old river banks.
  One time in the grass
  I stepped on an ass
And heard a young girl murmur: "Thanks!"

5

There was a young lady of Lynn,
Who was nothing but bones except skin.
  So she wore a false bust
  In the foolish false trust
That she looked like a woman of sin.

6

There was a young man from Racine,
Who invented a ****ing machine.
  Concave or convex
  To suit either sex—
The God-damnedest thing ever seen.

7

On May Day the girls of Penzance,
Being bored by a lack of romance,
  Joined the workers' parade
  With this banner displayed:
"What the Pants of Penzance Need Is Ants."

8

There was a young man from Ostend,
Who let a girl play with his end.
  She took hold of his Rover
  And felt it all over—
And did what she didn't intend.

9

A fellow whose surname was Hunt
Trained his tool to perform a slick stunt:
  This versatile spout
  Could be turned inside out
Like a glove, and be used as a ****.

10

There was a young fellow called Chick
Who fancied himself rather slick.
He went to a ball
Dressed in nothing at all
But a big velvet bow round his p***k.

11

A beautiful lady named Psyche
Was loved by a fellow named Ikey.
One thing about Ike
The lady can't like
Is his p***k, which is dreadfully spikey.

12

A chap down in old Oklahoma
Had a c**k that could sing La Paloma;
But the sweetness of pitch
Couldn't put off the hitch
Of impotence, size and aroma.

13

A broken-down harlot named Tupps
Was heard to confess in her cups:
  "The height of my folly
  Was ****ing a collie—
Though I got a nice price for the pups."

14

There was a gay parson of Tooting,
Whose roe he was frequently shooting;
  Till he married a lass
  With a face like my ass,
And a **** you could put a top boot in.

15

"The testes are cooler outside,"
Said the doc to the curious bride,
  "For the semen must not
  Get too ****ing hot,
And the bag fans your bum on the ride."

16

There once was a handsome young seaman,
Who with women was truly a demon:
    In peace or in war,
    At sea or on shore,
He could certainly dish out the semen.

17

A complacent old don of Divinity
Made boast of his daughter's virginity.
    They must have been dawdlin'
    Down at old Magdalen—
It couldn't have happened at Trinity.

18

There died an old man of Moldavia,
Well known for his bawdy behaviour.
    When the priest thought him shriven
    And fitted for heaven,
He cried: "Go and bugger the Saviour!"

19

A newly wed couple from Goshen
Spent their honeymoon sailing the ocean.
  In twenty-eight days
  They got laid eighty ways—
Imagine such ****ing devotion!

20

There once was a gay young Parisian,
Who screwed an appendix incision.
  But the girl of his choice,
  Could hardly rejoice
At this horrible work of precision.

21

Three lustful young sisters called Simms
Were endowed with over-size q***s.
  The Bishop of their Diocese
  Got elephantiasis—
His life wasn't all prayers and hymns!

22

When Theocritus guarded his flock
He piped in the shade of a rock.
  It is said that his Muse
  Was one of the ewes,
With a bum like a pink hollyhock.

23

An innocent maiden of Clewer
Incited her boy-friend to screw her.
  She tried to say no
  A half-second slow—
Now when she sits down she cries: "Oo-er!"

24

There was a young girl who begat
Three brats, by name Nat, Pat, and Tat.
  It was fun in the breeding,
  But hell in the feeding—
For she found she had no tit for Tat.

25

There were two Greek girls from Miletus,
Who said: "We wear gadgets that treat us,
When strapped on the thigh,
Up cosy and high,
To constant, convenient coitus."

26

Said a madam named Mamie la Farge
To a sailor just off of a barge:
"We have one girl that's dead,
With a hole in her head—
Of course there's a slight extra charge."

27

There was a young virgin named Alice,
Who thought of her **** as a chalice.
One night, sleeping nude,
She awoke feeling lewd,
And found in her chalice a phallus.

28

Said a dainty young whore named Miss Meggs:
"The men like to spread my two legs;
Then slip in between,
If you know what I mean,
And leave me the white of their eggs."

29

In the city of York there's a lass
Who will hitch up her skirts as you pass.
If you toss up two bits
She will strip to the tits
And let you explore her bare ass.

30

There was a young girl of Mobile,
Whose hymen was made of chilled steel:
To give her a thrill
Took a rotary drill
Or a Number Nine emery wheel.

31

There was a young pessimist, Grotton,
Who wished he had ne'er been begotten.
  Nor would he have been,
  But the rubber was thin,
And right at the tip it was rotten.

32

There is a young girl in New York,
Who is cautious for fear of the stork.
  You will find she is taped
  To prevent being raped,
And her ass-hole is plugged with a cork.

33

A certain young person of Ghent,
Uncertain if lady or gent,
  Shows his organs at large,
  For a small handling charge,
To assist him in paying the rent.

34

Please pity two young men of Perth,
Who had crabs, clap and syphilis from birth.
Said one to the other:
"We got this from mother;
We're the rottenest ****ers on earth."

35

A bishop whose See was Vermont
Used to toss himself off in the font.
The baptistry stank
With an odour most rank,
And no one would sit up in front.

36

Then up spake the Bey of Algiers,
And said to his harem: "My dears,
I know what you're expecting,
With your clitoris erecting—
But this morning 'twill be up your rears."

37

A talented ***stress, Miss Chisholm,
Was renowned for a fine paroxysm.
While the man detumesced,
She still spent with zest—
Her rapture sheer anachronism.

38

Have you heard of the Widow O'Reilly,
Who esteemed her late husband so highly,
That in spite of the scandal
Her umbrella handle
Was made of his membrum virile.

39

There was a fat man from Rangoon,
Whose thing was just like a balloon.
He tried hard to ride her
And when finally inside her
She thought she was pregnant too soon.

40

A major with wonderful aplomb
Called out in Hyde Park for a bum:
   Though he looked all around,
   Not one could be found—
So he just rhododendron, by gum!

41

An ingenious young man in Southend
Made a synthetic bum for a friend.
   But the friend shortly found
   Its construction unsound:
It was simply a bother—no end!

42

There was a young girl from Moline,
Whose technique was sweet and obscene.
   She would work on a p***k
   With every known trick,
And cleverly wink it quite clean.

43

There was a strong man of Drumrig,
Who one day did fifteen times frig;
  Then buggered three sailors,
  Two grocers, four tailors—
And ended by mounting a pig.

44

A Shah of the Empire of Persia
Lay for days in a sexual merger.
  When the nautch asked the Shah:
  "Won't you ever withdraw?"
e replied with a yawn: "It's inertia."

45

Meet Elmer, young son of the Thorpes,
Afflicted with psychotic warps.
  His idea of fun
  Is to bugger a nun,
And then vomit all over the corpse.

46

There once was a priest of Gibraltar,
Who wrote dirty jokes in his psalter.
  An inhibited nun,
  Who had read every one,
Made a vow to be laid on his altar.

47

A bishop of Winchester Junction
Found his phallus would no longer function.
  So in black crêpe he wound it,
  Tied a lily around it,
And solemnly gave it last unction.

48

There was an old maid from Van Nuys,
Who had a craze for making mud pies:
  She would fill them with farts,
  And pickled beef hearts,
And bake them between her fierce thighs.

49

There was a young girl whose divinity
Preserved her in perfect virginity;
'Till a candle, her nemesis,
Caused parllemogenesis—
Now she thinks herself one of the Trinity.

50

In Stokes lived an ugly bluestocking,
Who declared the men's manners were shocking.
Why, she'd never been diddled,
Even fingered or fiddled—
In the end she moved over to Focking.

51

There was a young fellow named Bream,
Who invented a wanking machine.
On the ninety-ninth stroke
The ****ing thing broke,
And ground his knackers to cream.

52

A Sultan of old Istanbul
Had nodules and warts on his tool:
  This evoked joyous grunts
  From his harem of ****s—
But his boys suffered badly at stool.

53

There was a young girl of Asturias,
Whose temper was frantic and furious.
  She used to throw tarts
  At her mate's private parts—
A habit unpleasant, but curious.

54

There was an old fellow named Skinner
Whose rod, it was said, had grown thinner.
  But still, by and large,
  He could always discharge,
Once he could just get it in her.

55

There was a young fellow named Paul,
Who confessed: "I have only one ball.
    But the size of my p***k
    Is God's dirtiest trick;
For the girls always ask: 'Is that all?' "

56

There was a young lady whose thighs
When spread showed a cave of such size,
    And so deep and so wide
    You could play cards inside—
Much to her bridegroom's surprise.

57

An old maid in the land of Aloha
Was wrapped in the coils of a boa:
    And as the snake squeezed,
    The old girl, not displeased,
Cried: "Darling! I love it! Samoa!"

58

A pathetic old maid of Bordeaux
Fell in love with a dashing young beau.
  To arrest his regard
  She would squat in his yard
And appealingly pee in the snow.

59

There was a young lady named Gager
Who, as the result of a wager,
  Consented to fart
  The whole oboe part
Of Mozart's Quartet in F Major.

60

There was a bold fellow named Wyatt,
Who kept a big girl on the quiet;
  And down on a wharf
  He kept also a dwarf,
In case he should go on a diet.

61

A clergyman up in Vermont
Keeps a goldfish alive in the font.
  When he dips the babes in,
  It tickles their skin—
Which is all that the innocents want.

62

If coitus gives one thrombosis
While continence causes neurosis,
  I prefer to expire
  Fulfilling desire
Than live on in a state of psychosis.

63

Of a sudden the great prima donna
Cried: "God, but my voice is a goner!"
  But a cat in the wings
  Said: "I know how she sings,"
And finished the solo with honour.

64

The King named Oedipus Rex,
Who started a fuss about sex,
  Put the world to great pains
  By the spots and the stains
Which he made on his mother's pubex.

65

A sprightly young tart in Pompeii
Used to make fifty drachma per day;
  But age dimmed her renown
  So that now she lies down
Fifty times for the same pay.

66

There was an old man of New York
Whose tool was as dry as a cork.
  While attempting to screw
  He split it in two—
Now he uses his tool as a fork.

67

Said a lively young nurse out in Padua
To her master: "Please, sir, you're a Dadua.
I've come down for some pins
For to wrap up the twins,
And to hear you remark, sir, how Gladua."

68

There was a young fellow from Lille,
Who enjoyed a good screw with a meal;
But once after mince pies
He'd had a surprise
He contented himself with a feel.

69

There was a young lady of Thun,
Who was blocked by the Man in the Moon.
"Well, it has been great fun,"
She remarked when he'd done,
"But I'm sorry you came quite so soon."

70

There was an old man of Corfu,
Who fed upon ****juice and spew:
  When he couldn't get that
  He ate what he shat—
And mighty good s**t he shat too.

71

There was a young lady of Munich,
Who was had in a park by a eunuch.
  In a moment of passion
  He shot her a ration
From a squirter concealed in his tunic.

72

There was an old woman of Orry,
Who went for a piss in a quarry.
  She knelt on a sack
  And opened her crack—
And a fellow backed in with a lorry.

73

Quoth a coroner's jury in Preston:
"The verdict is rectal congestion."
　They found an eight-ball
　Plus a shoemaker's awl
Half way up the major's intestine.

74

Any whore whose door sports a red light
Knows a whang when she sees one all right.
　She can tell by a glance
　At the drape of men's pants
If they are worth taking on for the night.

75

There was a young woman of Norway,
Who drove a rare trade in the whore way.
　Till a sodomite Viscount
　Brought **** to a discount
And the bawdy house belles to a poor way.

76

Two roosters in one of our pens
Found their p***ks were no larger than wens.
As they looked at their foreskins
And wished they had more skins,
They discovered they had both become hens.

77

An eccentric young poet, Silas Brown,
Raised up his embroidered gown.
To look for his peter
To beat it to metre,
But fainted—for nothing was found.

78

In the speech of the time did the Bard
Refer to his pud as his "yard";
But sigh no more, madams,
'Twas no longer than Adam's,
Or mine, and not one half as hard.

79

An aesthete from South Carolina
Had a c**k that tinkled like china.
    But while shooting his load
    It cracked like a spode,
So he bought it a matching vagina.

80

There was an old man of Madras,
Whose balls were made of brass:
    In stormy weather
    They'd all clang together,
Causing sparks to fly from his arse.

81

There was a young fellow of Strensall,
Whose pecker was just like a pencil.
    On the night of his wedding
    It went through the bedding
And shattered a chamber utensil.

82

So here was this fellow of Strensall,
Whose pecker was just like a pencil.
Anaemic 'tis true,
But an interesting screw,
In as much as the tip was prehensile.

83

There once was a party of negroes
In a land where the coconut tree grows.
Said one: "I must say,
After ****ing all day,
I find that my sense of fatigue grows."

84

There was a young man of Stamboul,
Who boasted so torrid a tool,
That each female crater
Explored by this satyr
Seemed almost unpleasantly cool.

85

A young man from the banks of the Po
Found his cock had elongated so
  That when he'd pee
  It was not so much he
But only his neighbours who'd know.

86

A Salvation lassie named Claire
Was having her first love affair.
  As she climbed into bed,
  She reverently said:
"I wish to be opened with prayer."

87

There once was a sacred baboon
That lived by the river Rangoon.
  And all of the women
  That choose to go swimmin'
He'd screw by the light of the moon.

88

There was an old hag named Le Sueur,
Who just was an out and out whore.
Between her big tits
You could come for two bits,
And she'd **** in any old sewer.

89

There was a young squaw of Wohunt,
Who possessed a collapsible ****.
It had many odd uses,
Produced no papooses,
And fitted both giant and runt.

90

In all of the Grecian metropolis
There was only one virgin—Papopoulos.
But her **** was all callous
From ****ing the phallus
Of a God who adorned the Acropolis.

91

There was a young fellow from Yale,
Whose face was exceedingly pale.
He spent his vacation
In self-stimulation
Because of the high price of tail.

92

The delighted incredulous bride
Remarked to the groom at her side.
"I never could quite
Believe till tonight
Our anatomies could coincide."

93

To a fancy-dress ball in Australia
Went a lady dressed up as a dahlia.
But when the leaves peeled
There was so much revealed
That the dress—as a dress—was a failure.

94

There once was a fellow named Fogg,
Who attempted to bugger a hog.
  While engaged in these frolics
  The hog ate his bollics—
And now he's a eunuch, by God!

95

While spending the winter at Pau
Lady Pamela forgot to say no;
  So the head porter made her,
  The chief barman laid her,
And the waiters were all hanging low.

96

There once was a maid in Duluth,
A striver and seeker for Truth.
  This pretty wench
  Was adept at French
And said all else was uncouth.

97

There was a young fellow named Howell,
Who buggered himself with a trowel.
He said that its shape
Was conducive to rape,
And could easily be cleaned with a towel.

98

A habit obscure and bizarre
Has taken a hold of Papa:
He brings home young camels
And other odd mammals
And gives them a go at Mamma.

99

A randy old rake from Stamboul
Felt his ardour grow suddenly cool.
No lack of affection
Reduced his erection
But his zipper had caught in his tool.

100

There once was a clergyman's daughter,
Who detested the pony he bought her.
  Till she found that its dong
  Was as hard and as long
As the prayers her father had taught her.

101

There was a young fellow named Tucker
Who, instructing a novice French sucker,
  Said: "Don't blow out your lips
  Like an elephant's hips;
The boys like them best when they pucker."

102

A remarkable race are the Persians,
They have such peculiar diversions.
  They screw the whole day
  In the regular way
And save up the nights for perversions.

103

There was a young chick from Brazil,
Who ****ed like a veritable mill.
   There was never a whore
   When she'd finished her chore
More prompt to present you her bill.

104

A medical student named Hettrick
Is learned in matters obstetric.
   From a glance at the toes
   Of the mother, he knows
If the foetus's balls are symmetric.

105

The nephew of one of the Tzars
Use to play with Rasputin at Yars:
   But the peasants revolted,
   The Romanovs bolted—
Now they're under the sickle and stars.

106

There was a young man from East Wubley,
Who prick was bifurcated doubly.
  Each quadruplicate shaft,
  Had two balls hanging aft—
The general effect was quite lovely.

107

There was a young lady from Thrace,
Whose corsets got too tight to lace.
  Her mother said: "Nelly,
  There's more in your belly
Than ever got in by your face."

108

There was a young man of Jesus,
Who performed cheap abortions with tweezers.
  One night in a hunt
  Up a mummified ****
He discovered the testes of Caesar.

109

There was a young fellow named Grimes
Who rogered his girl scores of times
  In the course of a week;
  And that's not to speak
Of assorted venereal crimes.

110

"Far dearer to me than my treasure,"
The heiress declared, "is my leisure.
  For then I can screw
  The whole Harvard crew.
They're slow, but that lengthens the pleasure."

111

There was a young lady of Pecking,
Who indulged in a great deal of necking.
  This seemed a great waste
  Since she claimed to be chaste—
This statement however needs checking.

112

There was a young miss from Johore,
Who'd lie on a mat on the floor.
  In a manner uncanny
  She'd wobble her fanny
And drain your nuts dry to the core.

113

There was a young girl from Des Moines,
Who had a large sack full of coins.
  The nickels and dimes
  She got from the times
That she cradled the boys in her loins.

114

There was a young lady named Mabel,
Who liked to sprawl out on a table.
  Then cry to her man:
  "Stuff in all you can—
Get both your balls in, if you're able!"

115

There was a young man of Seattle,
Who bested a bull in a battle.
  Without any compunction
  He assumed the bull's function
And deflowered a whole herd of cattle.

116

There was an old person of Delhi
Who awoke with a pain in his belly.
  And to cure it, 'twas said,
  He s**t in his bed—
The sheets were uncommonly smelly.

117

A rooster residing in Spain
Used to diddle his hens in the rain:
  "I give them a bloody
  Good time when it's muddy,
Which keeps them from getting too vain."

118

There once was a Vassar B.A.,
Who pondered the problem all day
  Of what there could be
  If C-*-*-T
Was divided by C-*-*-K.

119

A young Ph.D passing by
She gave him the problem to try.
  He worked the division
  With perfect precision
And the answer was B-A-B-Y.

120

There was a young girl from Decatur,
Who was ****ed by an old alligator.
  No one ever knew
  If she relished that screw,
For after he ****ed her, he ate her.

121

Said a lovely young lady named Lake
Pervertedly fond of a snake:
  "If my dear friend, the boa
  Shoots spermatozoa,
What offspring we'll leave in our wake."

122

Then up spake an old Chinese mandarin:
"There's a subject I'd like to use candour in:
  The geese in Pekin
  Are so steeped in sin
They'd as soon let a man as a gander in."

123

No one can tell about Myrtle
Whether she's steril' or fertil'.
  If anyone tries
  To tickle her thighs,
She closes them tight like a turtle.

124

There was a young woman in Dee,
Who peed like a man she did see.
  When it came to a test
  She wished to be best,
And practice makes perfect, you see.

125

There was a young girl from New York,
Who plugged up her **** with a cork.
  A woodpecker or two
  Made the grade, it is true—
But it totally baffled the stork.

126

Till along came a man who presented
A tool that was strangely indented.
  With a dazzling twirl
  He penetrated that girl—
And thus was the corkscrew invented.

127

If Leo your own birthday marks
You will lust until forty, when starts
  A new pleasure in stamps
  Boy Scouts and their camps,
And fondling nude statues in parks.

128

A visitor once to Loch Ness
Met the monster, who left him a mess.
  They returned his entrails
  By the regular mails,
And his genitals went by express.

129

A cross-eyed old painter McNeff
Was colour-blind, palsied, and deaf.
  When he asked to be touted
  The critics all shouted:
"This is art, with a capital F!"

2—TWAFM • •

130

A rascal far gone in lechery
Lured maids to their ruin by his treachery.
He invited them in
For the purpose of sin—
Though he said 'twas to look at his etchery.

131

A lassie from wee Ballachulish
Observed: "Och, virginity's foolish.
When a lad makes a try
To say ought but Aye!
Is stubborn, pig-headed and mulish."

132

There was a young chappie named Cyril
Who was had in a wood by a squirrel,
And he liked it so good
That he stayed in the wood
Just as long as the squirrel stayed viril'.

133

A strip-teaser up in Fall River
Caused a sensitive fellow to quiver.
  The aesthetic vibration
  Brought ecstatic elation—
Besides, it was good for his liver.

134

A whore grown too old to get laid
Turned *parfumeuse,* finding it paid
  To concoct *Fleur de Floozie*
  From the juice of her pussy—
"Substantial discount to the trade."

135

Thus spake a young monk of La Trappe,
Who had a fierce dose of the clap:
  "*Dominus vobiscum.*
  Why don't my piss come?
There's something gone wrong with the tap."

136

There was an old man of Cajon,
Who never could get a good bone.
  With the aid of a gland
  It grew simply grand—
Now his wife cannot leave it alone.

137

There was a young man, a Maltese,
Who could even screw horses with ease.
  He'd flout natural laws
  In this manner because
Of his dong, which hung down to his knees.

138

There was a young lady from Deal,
Who was raped in a lake by an eel.
  One morning at dawn
  She gave birth to a prawn,
Two crabs and a small baby seal.

139

There was a young lady of Rheims,
Who amazingly pissed in four streams.
  Till her pal poked around
  And a fly-button found
Wedged tightly in one of her seams.

140

There was an old man of Duluth,
Whose c**k was shot off in his youth.
  He ****ed with his nose
  And with fingers and toes
And he came through a hole in his tooth.

141

There was an old Scot, McTavish,
Who attempted an anthropoid ravish.
  The object of rape
  Was the wrong sex of ape
And the anthropoid ravished McTavish,

142

"Last night," said a lassie called Ruth,
"In a long-distance telephone booth,
I enjoyed the perfection
Of an ideal connection—
I was screwed, if you must know the truth."

143

A lady with features cherubic
Was famed for her area pubic.
When they asked her its size
She replied in surprise:
"Are you speaking of square feet, or cubic?"

144

A team playing baseball in Dallas
Called the umpire "s**t!" out of malice.
While this worthy had fits,
The team made eight hits,
And a girl in the bleachers called Alice.

145

There once was a family called Doe,
A fine friendly family to know.
As father screwed mother,
She said: "You're bigger than brother."
And he said: "Yes, sis told me so!"

146

A clever individual called Krupp
Wore a belt when he wanted to tup.
His mighty dry cells
Made his balls buzz like bells
And lighted the whole entrance up.

147

A prudish young damsel named Rose
Is particular how men propose.
To: "Let's have intercourse,"
She says: "But of course".—
But to "Let's ****," she turns up her nose.

148

A hot-tempered girl of Caracas
Was wed to a samba-mad jackass.
  When he started to cheat her
  With a dark senorita
She kicked him right in the maracas.

149

There was an old fellow from Croydon
Whose cook was a cute little hoyden.
  She would sit on his knees
  While shelling the peas
Or pleasanter duties employed on.

150

There was a young lady named Etta,
Who fancied herself in a sweater.
  Three reasons she had—
  To keep warm was not bad,
But the other two reasons were better.

151

There was a young lady named Grace,
Who had eyes in a very odd place.
 She could sit on the hole
 Of a mouse or a mole
And stare the beast square in the face.

152

A flatulent nun of Hawaii
One Easter eve supped on papaya,
 Then honoured the Passover
 By turning her arse over
And obliging with Handel's "Messiah".

153

There was a young fellow named Lancelot
Whom his neighbours all looked on askance a lot
 Whenever he'd pass
 An attractive young lass
The front of his pants would advance a lot.

154

To Sadie the touch of a male meant
An emotional cardiac ailment,
   And acuteness of breath
   Caused her untimely death
In the course of erotic impalement.

155

There was a young man called Pat,
The cheeks of whose arse were so fat
   That they had to be parted
   Whenever he farted,
And propped wide apart when he shat.

156

There was a young man from Montmartre,
Who was famed far and wide for his fart.
   When folk said: "What a noise!"
   He replied with smooth poise:
"When I fart, I fart from the heart."

157

The sex of the asteroid vermin
Is exceedingly hard to determine.
The galactic patrol
Simply ****s any hole
That will possibly let all the sperm in.

158

There was an old ostler named Raines,
Possessed more of ballocks than brains.
He stood on a stool
To bugger a mule
And got kicked in the balls for his pains.

159

There was a young lady named Schneider,
Who often kept trysts with a spider.
She found a strange bliss
In the hiss of her piss
As it strained through the cobwebs inside her.

160

A musicienne, Gay Montebello,
Amused herself playing a cello;
But not really a solo
For she would use as a bow
The dong of a sturdy young fellow

161

There was a young angel named Rayloe,
Around whose arse shone a halo.
When asked its intent
He replied, as he bent,
"It sanctifies those who would play low."

162

There was an Old Man of the Mountain,
Who tossed himself into a fountain.
Fifteen times though he spent,
Still he wasn't content—
He simply got tired of the counting.

163

There was a young rake of Penzance,
Who rogered his three maiden aunts.
  Though he defiled 'em,
  He never "with-child'd" 'em
Through using the letters of France.

164

A young fellow whose sight was myopic
Thought sex an incredible topic
  So poor were his eyes
  That in spite of its size
His penis appeared microscopic.

165

There was a young man from Racine,
Who was weaned at the age of sixteen.
  He said: "I'll admit,
  There's no milk in the tit;
But think of the fun that it's been."

166

On his honeymoon sailing the ocean
A tightwad displayed much emotion
  When he learned one fine day
  He'd been ****ing away
What could have been bottled as lotion.

167

There was a young man named Murray,
Who made love to his girl in a surrey.
  She started to sigh
  But someone walked by,
So he buttoned his pants in a hurry.

168

There once was a gay young Parisian,
Who came to an awful decision.
  For his sexual joys
  He'd have women and boys,
And rabbits—without supervision!

169

A keen-scented dean of Tacoma
Was awarded a special diploma
  For his telling apart
  Of a masculine fart
From a similar female aroma.

170

There was an old whore of Algiers,
Who had bushels of dirt in her ears.
  The tip of her titty
  Was remarkably s**tty—
She couldn't have washed it for years.

171

There was an old codger named Wright,
Who did nasty things just for spite.
  He knocked up his daughter
  And then tried to abort her
By biting her tits in the night.

172

There was a young fellow named Charted,
Who rubbed soap on his bung when it smarted;
 And to his surprise
 He received a grand prize
For the bubbles he blew when he farted.

173

There was a young lady of Riga,
Who smiled as she rode on a tiger.
 They continued the ride
 With the lady inside
And a smile on the face of the tiger.

174

There was a young lady of Whitby,
Who had the bad luck to be bit by
 Two little brown things
 Without any wings
Right on the place she must sit by.

175

There was a young man of high station,
Who was found by a pious relation
   Making love in a ditch
   To—I won't say a bitch—
But, well, a woman of no reputation.

176

There was a young lady from Sydney,
Who took it right up to her kidney.
   But a man from Quebec
   Shoved it up to her neck—
He had a long one, now didn't he?

177

A virile young man of Jourdaine
Had vesicles no one could drain.
   With an unbroken flow
   Round the course he would go,
Then roll over and start in again.

178

A fisherman off of Cape Cod
Said: "I'll bugger that tuna, by God!"
But the high-minded fish
Resented his wish
And nimbly swam off with his rod.

179

There was a young lady of Rhodes,
Who sinned in unusual modes.
At the height of her fame
She abruptly became
The mother of four slimy toads.

180

There was an old man of Boolong,
Who frightened the birds with his song.
It wasn't the words
That frightened the birds,
But the horrible *dooble ong-tong*.

181

"I'll admit," said a lady named Starr,
"That a phallus is like a cigar:
But to a most common people
A phallic church steeple
Is stretching the matter too far."

182

I love her in her evening gown.
I love her in her nightie.
But when moonlight flits
Between her tits—
Phew!—Jesus Christ Almighty!

183

There was a young fellow named Falls,
Who was famous in old Music Halls:
His favourite trick
Was to spin on his p***k
And then roll off the stage on his balls.

184

There was a young woman named Dottie,
Who said as she sat on her potty:
  "It isn't polite
  To do this in sight—
But then, who am I to be snottie?"

185

A talented fellow from Sparta
Displayed rare skill as a farter.
  From the power of one bean
  He could fart: "God Save the Queen"
And Beethoven's "Moonlight Sonata".

186

He was great in the Christmas Cantata;
He could double-stop fart the Toccata;
  He'd boom from his ass
  Bach's B-minor Mass,
And in counterpoint, La Traviata.

187

There was a young man of Toulouse,
Who thought he would diddle a goose.
He hunted and bunted
To get the thing ****ed,
Then shrugged and declared: "It's no use!"

188

A sailor indulged in coitus
With a cow of the genus Cetus.
Piscatologists thundered,
Biologists wondered,
At the anchor tattooed on the foetus.

189

There was an old man of Ramnugger,
Who raised a fair trade as a bugger.
Till a fair young Circassian
Brought ****ing in fashion
And spoiled all the buggery in Ramnugger.

190

Now first he got acne vulgaris,
The kind that is rampant in Paris.
  It covered his skin
  From forehead to shin
And now people ask where his hair is.

191

With symptoms increasing in number,
His aorta's in need of a plumber.
  His heart is cavorting,
  His wife is aborting,
And now he's acquired a gumma.

192

Consider his terrible plight—
His eyes won't react to the light,
  His hands are apraxic,
  His gait is ataxic,
He's developing gun-barrel sight.

193

His passions are strong, as before,
But his penis is flaccid and sore;
His wife now has tabes
And sabre-toothed babies—
She's really worse off than a whore.

194

There are pains in his belly and knees,
His sphincters have gone by degrees:
Paroxysmal incontinence,
With all its concomitants,
Bring one quite unpredictable pees.

195

Though treated in every known way,
His spirochetes grow day by day.
He's developed paresis,
Converses with Jesus,
And calls himself "Queen of the May."

196

There was a young lady named Mabel.
Who would screw on a bed or a table.
  Though a two-dollar screw
  Was the best she could do,
Her arse bore a ten-dollar label.

197

An unfortunate maiden was Esther,
A peculiar repugnance possessed her:
  A reaction compulsive
  Made kissing repulsive,
Which was rough on those who caressed her.

198

There was a young fellow named Hammer
Who had an unfortunate stammer.
  "The b-bane of my life,"
  Said he, "is my wife.
D-d-d-d-d-d-damn 'er!"

199

A prolific young mother named Hall,
Who seemed to have triplets each Fall,
When asked why and wherefore
Said: "That's what we're here for—
But we often get nothing at all."

200

There was a young damsel named Jinx,
Who when asked what she thought of the
Sphinx,
Replied with a smile:
"That old fraud by the Nile?
I personally think that he stinks."

201

There was a young lady named Lily,
With a craving to walk Piccadilly:
Said she: "Ain't it funny,
It's not for the money—
But if I don't take it, it's silly."

202

Astute Melanesians on Munda
Heard a padre discussing the wunda
Of Virginal Birth:
They debated its worth,
Then tore the poor padre asunda.

203

There was a young maid of Odessa,
A somewhat unblushing transgressor.
When sent to the priest
The lewd little beast
Began to undress her confessor.

204

A plumpish young lady of Eton,
Whose delight was to read Mrs. Beeton,
Said: "Marry me, Jack
And you'll find that my crack
Is a nice place to warm your cold feet on."

205

She married a fellow called Tony,
Who soon found her screwing the pony.
Said he: "What's it got,
My dear, that I've not?"
Sighed she: "Just a yard-long bologna."

206

A disgusting young man named McGill
Made his neighbours exceedingly ill
When they heard of his habits
Involving white rabbits
And a bird with a flexible bill.

207

There was a young girl from Cape Cod,
Who thought her child came from God.
It wasn't the Almighty
Who lifted her nightie,
But Roger, the lodger, the sod!

208

There was a young girl from Kildare,
Who once was attacked by a bear.
  While chased in a field
  She tripped and revealed
Some meat to the bear that was rare.

209

There was a young girl from New York,
Who diddled herself with a cork.
  It stuck in her vagina—
  Can you imagina
Her pulling it out with a fork?

210

The eminent Mrs. La Rue
Was born in a cage at the zoo.
  And the curious rape
  Which made her an ape
Is highly fantastic, if true.

211

Said a charming young lady of Padua,
"A peso! Oh, sir, what a cadua!"
He said, lifting his hat,
"You ain't even worth that.
However, I'm glad to have hadua."

212

There was a young chappie named Price,
Who dabbled in all sorts of vice.
He had virgins and boys
And mechanical toys—
And on Mondays, he meddled with mice!

213

A naked young tart named Giselle
Walked the streets while ringing a bell.
When asked why she rang it
She answered: "God dang it!
Can't you see I have something to sell?"

214

There was a young lady named Smith
Whose virtue was mostly a myth.
  She said: "Try as I can
  I just can't find a man
Who is fun to be virtuous with."

215

Three lovely young girls from St. Thomas
Attended dance halls in pyjamas.
  They were fondled all summer
  By sax, bass, and drummer—
I'm surprised that by now they're not mamas.

216

There was a young fellow named Willie,
Who acted remarkably silly:
  At an All-Nations ball
  Dressed in nothing at all
He claimed that his costume was Chile.

217

There was a young maiden of Gloucester
Whose parents were sure they had lost her,
    Till they came in the grass
    To the marks of her ass
And the knees of the man who had crossed her.

218

There was a young lady named Maud,
Who was a society fraud:
    In the drawing-room she
    Was as staid as could be—
But out in the garden . . . Oh! Lord!

219

There was a young farmer of Nant,
Whose conduct was both gay and gallant.
    For he ****ed all his dozens
    Of nieces and cousins,
In addition, of course, to his aunt.

220

There was an old man of Tantivy,
Who followed his son to the privy.
He lifted the lid
To see what he did,
And found that it smelt of Capivi.

221

There was a young lady of Crewe,
Whose cherry a chap had got through.
When told to her mother
She fixed up another
Out of rubber and red ink and glue.

222

There was a young lady of Rheims,
Who was terribly plagued by wet dreams.
So she saved up a dozen
To send to her cousin—
He ate them and thought they were creams.

223

There's a pretty young lady named Sark
Afraid to get laid in the dark.
    But she's often mishandled
    By the light of a candle
In the bushes of Gramercy Park

224

A widow whose singular vice
Was to keep her late husband on ice
    Said: "It's been hard since I lost him
    But I'll never defrost him—
Cold comfort, but cheap at the price."

225

Concerning the bees and the flowers
In the fields and the gardens and bowers:
    You will note at a glance
    That their ways of romance
Are totally different from ours.

226

There was a young man of high station
Attached to the Chinese Legation.
    He liked to be ****ed
    And adored being sucked—
But he revelled in pure masturbation.

227

There was a small boy of Quebec,
Who was buried in snow to his neck.
    When asked: "Are you friz?"
    He answered: "I is!
But we don't call this cold in Quebec."

228

There was a gay person of Tooting,
Whose roe was frequently shooting.
    Thrice he married a lass
    With a face like my ass
And a **** you could put a top boot in.

229

A young man of Newminster Court
Buggered a pig, but his rod was too short.
  Said the hog: "It's not nice,
  But pray take my advice:
Make tracks or by the police you'll be caught."

230

There once was a fellow from Beverly,
Who went in for ****ing quite heavily.
  He ****ed night and day
  Till his bollocks gave way—
But the doctors replaced them quite cleverly.

231

A young man maintained that his trigger
Was so big there weren't any bigger.
  But this long and thick pud
  Was so heavy it could
Scarcely lift up its head. It lacked vigour.

232

There was a young fellow named Pete,
Who was gentle and shy and discreet;
  But with his first woman
  He became quite inhuman
And constantly roared for fresh meat.

233

The priests at the temple of Isis
Used to offer us amber and spices:
  Then back of the shrine
  They would play sixty-nine,
And other unmentionable vices.

234

A young schizophrenic named Struther
When told of the death of his mother,
  Said: "Yes, it's too bad,
  But I can't feel too sad—
After all, I still have each other."

235

There was a young girl from Hoboken,
Who claimed that her hymen was broken
From riding a bike
On a cobblestone pike—
But it really was broken from pokin'.

236

An assistant professor named Ddodd
Had manners arresting and odd.
He said: "If you please,
Spell my name with four 'd's'—
Though one was sufficient for God."

237

A young parson once lived in King's Lynn
Said he thought fornication was sin.
Till a girl said: "You fool,"
Went and whipped out his tool,
Took her drawers off and shoved his thing in.

238

The thoughts of the rabbit on sex
Are seldom, if ever, complex;
For a rabbit in need
Is a rabbit indeed,
And does just as a person expects.

239

An accident really uncanny
Befell a respectable granny:
She sat down in a chair
While her false teeth were there,
And bit herself right in the fanny.

240

A man who came into some money
Decided to marry a Bunny.
But the thought of the ears
And the tails of the dears
Made him dismiss the idea as just funny.

241

A girl by the green Susquehanna
Said she would do it manana.
    But her lover got sore
    And sailed off to Lahore—
And now she must use a banana.

242

There was a young parson of Goring,
Who made a small hole in the flooring.
    He lined it all round,
    Then laid on the ground,
And declared it much cheaper than whoring.

243

A thrifty old man named McEwan
Inquired: "Why be bothered with screwing?
    It's safer and neater
    To finger your peter—
And besides, you can see what you're doing."

244

There was a young fellow from Reading,
Who was constantly wetting the bedding.
  Till his wife had to say:
  "I don't mind the spray.
It's the stench in the morning I'm dreading."

245

There once was a rich old roué,
Who felt his life slipping away.
  He endowed a large ward
  In a house where he'd whored.
A large crowd at his funeral? I'll say.

246

The wife of a red-headed Celt
Lost the key to her chastity belt.
  She tried picking the lock
  With an Ulsterman's c**k;
And the next thing he knew he was gelt.

247

There was a young damsel named Carole,
Who liked to play stud for apparel.
  Her opponent's straight flush
  Brought a maidenly blush
And a hasty trip home in a barrel.

248

There was a young lady in Natchez,
Who peed in some nettle-thick patches.
  She sits in her room
  With her bare little moon
And scratches and scratches and scratches.

249

A girl of as graceful a mien
As ever in England was seen
  Stepped into a pub
  Hit a man with a club
And razored to shreds his machine.

250

There was a young fellow from Parma,
Who was solemnly screwing his charmer.
Said the damsel, demure,
"You'll excuse me, I'm sure.
But I must say you **** like a farmer."

251

A young girl of North Carolina
Had a very capricious vagina.
To the shock of the ****er
It would suddenly pucker
And render a chorus of "Dinah."

252

A highly aesthetic young Jew
Had eyes of a heavenly blue.
The end of his dillie
Was shaped like a lily,
And his balls were too utterly *two*.

253

I wooed a young nurse in Bermuda.
I was lewd, but by God! she was lewder.
  She said it was crude
  To be wooed in the nude—
I pursued her, subdued her, and screwed her!

254

There was a young lady of Lynn,
Who was deep in original sin.
  When told to be good
  She said: "Wish I could,"
And straightway went at it again.

255

A licentious old Justice of Salem
Used to catch all the harlots and jail 'em.
  But instead of a fine
  He would stand them in line
For his common-law tool to impale 'em.

256

All winter the eunuch from Munich
Went walking all day in his tunic.
  Folks said: "You've a cough
  And you'll freeze your balls off."
Said he: "That's why I'm a eunuch."

257

There once was a lady called Annie,
Who had lice, fleas, and crabs up her fanny.
  Getting up her flue
  Was like touring the zoo—
Wild beasts lurked in each nook and cranny.

258

There was a young man from Cadiz,
Who planted an acre of tits.
  They came up in the fall,
  Red nipples and all,
And he carefully chewed them to bits.

259

There was an old Chinaman, drunk,
Who went for a sail in his junk.
He was dreaming of Venus
And tickling his penis,
Till he floated away in the spunk.

260

A surly and pessimistic Druid,
A defeatist, if only he knew it,
Said: "The world's on the skids
And I think having kids
Is a waste of good seminal fluid."

261

There was a young lady from Slough,
Who said that she didn't know how.
Then a young fellow caught her
And jolly well taught her.
She lodges in Pimlico now.

262

There was a young fellow named Ringer,
Who was screwing an opera singer.
  Said he with a grin:
  "Well I've sure got it in."
Sang she: "You mean that's not your finger?"

263

There was a young laundress named Wrangle,
Whose tits tilted up at an angle.
  "That may tickle my chin"
  Said she, with a grin.
"But at least they keep out of the mangle."

264

There was a young fellow named Kane,
Who screwed some disgusting old Jane.
  She was ugly and smelly,
  With a ghastly pot belly;
But—well, they were caught in the rain.

265

There was a young man named McNamiter,
With a tool of prodigious diameter.
    But it wasn't the size
    Gave the girls a surprise,
But his rhythm—iambic pentameter.

266

A young man of Novorossisk
Had a mating procedure so brisk.
    With such super speed action
    The Lorentz contraction
Foreshortened his prick to a disk.

267

A young man with a passion quite vast
Used to talk about making it last,
    Till one day he discovered
    His sister uncovered,
And now he ****s often and fast.

268

There was a young Bishop from Brest,
Who openly practised incest.
  "My sisters and nieces
  Are all dandy pieces,
And they don't cost a cent," he confessed.

269

Have you heard of Professor McKay,
Who lays all the girls in the hay?
  Though he thinks it's romantic,
  He drives the girls frantic
By *talking* a wonderful lay.

270

There was a young man named Pete,
Who was more than a bit indiscreet.
  He pulled at his dong
  Until it grew long,
And actually dragged in the street.

271

All the lady-apes ran from King Kong,
For his dong was unspeakably long.
  But a friendly giraffe
  Quaffed his yard and a half
And ecstatically burst into song.

272

A virgin felt urged in Toulouse
Till she thought she would try self-abuse.
  In search of a hard'n
  She ran into a garden
And was had by a statue of Zeus.

273

There was a young monk from Dundee,
Who hung a nun's **** on a tree.
  He grabbed her fair ass
  And performed a high mass
That even the Pope came to see.

274

The last time I dined with the King,
He did quite a curious thing.
  He sat on a stool
  And took out his tool
And said: "If I play, will you sing?"

275

From the depth of the crypts at St. Giles
Came a scream that was heard for ten miles.
  "Oh, goodness gracious!"
  Cried Brother Ignatius
"I forgot that the Bishop had piles."

276

There was a young lady named Brent,
With a **** of enormous extent.
  It was so deep and so wide
  You could go camping inside,
Provided you brought your own tent.

277

There was an old man from Greenwich,
Whose balls hung down like spinach.
    His remarkable tool
    He kept wound on a spool
And unrolled it inich by inich.

278

There was a young fellow from Lynn,
Whose dong was the size of a pin.
    Said his girl with a laugh,
    As she felt of his staff:
"*This* won't be much of a sin."

279

An archaeologist fellow named Rossyl
Once found an unusual fossil.
    He could tell by the bend
    And the knob at the end
It was the peter of Paul the Apostle.

280

There was a young girl named Molly
Who thought all fornication folly.
   She'd say: "Your pee pee
   Means nothing to me,
But I'll do it just to be jolly."

281

There was a young prince Montezuma,
Who had an affair with a puma.
   The puma in play
   Clawed both balls away—
An example of animal humour.

282

There was a young girl from Korea,
Who liked sticking flutes up her rear.
   After eating escargots
   She could fart Handel's "Largo"
And encore with "Ave Maria."

283

There was a young man of Rangoon,
Who farted and filled a balloon.
  The balloon went so high
  That it stuck in the sky
And stank out the man in the moon.

284

There was a young girl named Arden,
Who was blowing her beau in the garden.
  When he asked, with a squirm:
  "What became of the sperm?"
She answered: (Gulp) "Beg pardon?"

285

There was an aesthetic young miss,
Who thought it the apex of bliss
  To jazz herself silly
  With the bud of a lily,
Then prance to the garden and piss.

286

There was a young man from Bombay,
Who moulded a **** out of clay.
  But the heat of his p***k
  Turned the clay into brick
And wore all his foreskin away.

287

There was a young fellow named Kimble,
Whose penis was exceedingly nimble.
  Both fragile and slender,
  And dainty and tender—
So he kept it encased in a thimble.

288

A lusty young buck from Lahore
Was asked: "When do you roger your whore?
  He said: "At eleven;
  At three, five, and seven;
Then at eight and a quarter past four."

289

A publisher once went to France
In search of a tale of romance.
  A Parisian lady
  Told a story so shady
That he immediately made an advance.

290

There was a young man from St. Pauls,
Who read *Harper's Bazaar* and *McCalls,*
  Till he grew such a passion
  For feminine fashion
That he knitted a snood for his balls.

291

There was a young cowboy named Gary,
Who was desperately anxious to marry.
  But he found the defection
  Of any erection
A difficult factor to parry.

292

Said a certain old Earl whom I knew:
"I've been struck from the rolls of *Who's Who*
   Just because I was found
   Lying prone on the ground
With the housemaid—and very nice too!"

293

Rosalind, a pretty young lass,
Had a truly delightful ass.
   No, not dimpled and pink,
   As you possibly think—
It was grey, had long ears, and ate grass.

294

There was a young girl of East Anglia,
Whose loins were a tangle of ganglia.
   Her mind was a webbing
   Of Freud and Kraftt-Ebing
And all sorts of other new fanglia.

295

When the White Man attempted to rule
The Indians made him look a fool.
They cut off his nuts
To hang in their huts
And stuffed up his mouth with his tool.

296

A famous theatrical actress
Played best in the role of malefactress;
Yet her home life was pure
Except, to be sure
A scandal or two just for practice.

297

In his youth our old friend Boccaccio
Was laying a girl in the patio.
When it came to the t**t
She wasn't so hot—
But, God!, was she good at fellatio!

298

A geologist, one Dr. Robb,
Found bothersome his thingamabob.
With a stroke of his pick
He knocked off his wick—
And calmly went on with his job.

299

There was a young lady called Brandon,
Whose feet were too narrow to stand on.
So she stood on her head,
"For my motto," she said,
"Has always been *Nil desperandum.*"

300

God's plan made a hopeful beginning
But man spoiled his chances by sinning.
We trust that the story
Will end in God's glory,
But at present the other side's winning.

301

Said a fancy-dress Lady of Shalott:
"I wish I had teeth in my t**t.
  For just think," said she,
  "How nice it would be
To keep all the p****s that I got."

302

A girl attending Bryn Mawr
Committed a dreadful *faux pas*:
  She loosened a stay
  In her decolleté
Exposing her *je-ne-sais-quoi*.

303

Said a certain nubile fair siren:
"Young sailors are cute—I must try one!"
  She came home in the nude,
  Stewed, screwed, and tattooed
With lewd pictures and verses by Byron.

304

A pious old lady named Tweak
Has taught her vagina to speak.
It is frequently liable
To quote from the bible,
But when ****ing—not even a squeak.

305

Though the invalid pious Saint Brac
Lay all of his life on his back,
His wife got her share
And the pilgrims now stare
At the scene, nicely shown, on a plaque.

306

Every time Lady Lowbodice swoons,
Her bubbies pop out like balloons;
But her butler stands by
With *hauteur* in his eye
And lifts them back in with warm spoons.

307

A signora who strolled down the Corso
Displayed quite a lot of her torso.
A crowd soon collected
And no one objected,
Though some were in favour of more so.

308

There was a young man had the art
Of making a capital tart
With a handful of ****
Some snot and some spit—
And he'd flavour the whole with a fart.

309

There was a young maid from Worcester,
Who dreamt a young man had seduced her.
She awoke with a scream
To find it a dream:
'Twas a bump in the mattress that had goosed her.

310

There was a young lady named May,
Who frigged herself long in the hay.
  She bought a pickle
  One for a nickel
And rubbed all her old warts away.

311

There was a young girl in Alsace,
Who was having her first piece of ass:
  "Oh, darling, you'll kill me;
  Oh, darling, you thrill me.
Like Father John's thumb after mass."

312

When a lecherous curate at Leeds
Was discovered one day in the weeds
  Astride a young nun,
  He said: "Christ, this is fun:
Far better than telling one's beads."

313

A young curate, just new to the cloth,
At sex was surely no sloth.
  He preached masturbation
  To his whole congregation,
And was washed down the aisle in the froth.

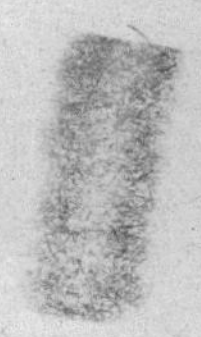

314

A milkmaid there was, with a stutter,
Who was badly in need of a futter.
  Having nowhere to turn
  She made use of a churn
And managed to come with the butter.

315

In Oregon a girl called Alice
Used T.N.T for a phallus:
  They found her vagina
  In North Carolina
And picked up her asshole in Dallas.

316

There were two young ladies of Birmingham
And this is a story concerning them.
  They lifted the frock
  And tickled the c**k
Of a parson as he was confirming 'em.

317

Now this parson was nobody's fool
He was taught in a large public school.
  He took down his britches
  And rogered the bitches
With his ten-inch episcopal tool.

318

A lively young maiden named Aird,
Whose bottom is always kept bared:
  When asked why, she pouts,
  And says the Boy Scouts
All beg her to please "Be Prepared".

319

There was a young fellow named Bill,
Who took an atomic pill:
His navel corroded,
His asshole exploded,
And they picked up his balls in Brazil.

320

There was a young girl from the coast,
Who had an affair with a ghost.
In the midst of a spasm
This smooth ectoplasm
Said: "It's wonderful, I can feel it—almost."

321

There was a young fellow named Dirkin,
Who was always jerkin' his gherkin.
His mother said: "Dirkin
Quit jerkin' your gherkin,
Your gherkin's for ferkin', not jerkin'."

322

A bather whose clothing was strewed
By winds that left her quite nude,
  Saw a man come along
  And unless we are wrong
You expected this line to be lewd.

323

There was a young fellow from Eno,
Who said to his girl: "Now old Beano,
  Lift your skirt up in front
  And enlarge your whole ****,
For the size of my organ is keen-o.

324

For sculpture that's really first class
You need form, composition, and mass.
  To do a good Venus
  Just leave out the penis
And concentrate all on the ass.

325

A sculptor remarked: "I'm afraid
I have fallen in love with my trade.
  I'm much too elated
  With what I've created,
And chiefly the women I've made."

326

There was an old man of Bubungi,
Whose balls were all covered with fungi,
  With his friends, out at lunch,
  He tore off a bunch,
Saying: "Now divide this among ye."

327

A cabby who drove in Biarritz
Once frightened a fare into fits.
  When reproved for a fart,
  He said: "God bless your heart;
When I break wind I usually ****s."

328

There was a young lady at sea
Who said: "How it hurts me to pee!"
"I see," said the mate,
"That accounts for the state
Of the captain, the purser, and me."

329

An amorous maiden antique
Locked a man in her house for a week;
He entered her door
With a shout and a roar—
But his exit was marked by a squeak.

330

There was a young lass of Dalkeith,
Who frigged a young man with her teeth.
She complained that he stunk
Not so much from the spunk,
But his ****hole was just underneath.

331

There was a young parson of Harwich
Tried to grind his betrothed in a carriage,
  She cried: "No, you young goose,
  Just try self-abuse—
The other will come after marriage."

332

There was a gay parson of Norton
Whose p***k, although slick, was a short 'un.
  To make up for this loss
  He had balls like a horse
And never spent less than a quartum.

333

Exuberant Sue from Anjou
Found that ****ing affected her hue.
  She presented to sight
  Some parts pink, some parts white,
And others quite purple and blue.

334

There was an old lady of Tring,
Who sat down by the fire to sing:
A piece of charcoal
Flew up her ****hole
And burned all the hairs off her thing.

335

There was a young man of Baghdad,
Who dreamed that he slept with a lad;
He dreamt he was spawning
And then in the morning
Woke up to find that he had.

336

An agreeable girl named Miss Doves
Likes to fondle the men that she loves.
She will use her bare fist
If the fellows insist,
But really she prefers to wear gloves.

337

A lady while living at Crewe
Found a large mouse in her stew.
  Said the waiter: "Don't shout,
  And don't wave it about,
Or the others will all want one too."

338

A young man by a girl was desired
To give her the thrills she required.
  But he died of old age
  Ere his rod could assuage
The volcanic desire it inspired.

339

There was a young damsel named Baker,
Who was poked in a pew by a Quaker.
  He cried: "What!
  Do you call this a t**t?
Why the entrance is more than an acre!"

340

A squeamish young fellow named Brand
Thought caressing his person was grand.
  But he viewed with distaste
  The gelatinous paste
That it left in the palm of his hand.

341

There once lived a Queen of Bulgaria
Whose bush had grown hairier and hairier.
  Once a Prince from Peru
  Who fancied a screw
Had to hunt for her fan with a terrier.

342

There was a young fellow named Fyfe
Whose marriage was ruined for life;
  For he had an aversion
  To every perversion
And only liked ****ing his wife.

343

Well, one year the poor woman struck,
And she wept and she cursed at her luck,
And she said: "Where have you gotten us
With your goddam monotonous
**** after **** after ***?"

344

A resolute Swede in Minneapolis
Discovered his sex life was hapless;
The more he would screw
The more he'd want to,
And he feared he would soon become sapless.

345

A sailor who slept in the sun
Woke to find his fly buttons undone.
He remarked with a smile:
"Stone me, a sundial!
I see it's a quarter past one."

346

There was a young lady named Brent
With a **** of enormous extent,
And so deep and so wide
The acoustics inside
Were so good you could hear when you spent.

347

Ah, Vienna, the fortress of Freud,
Whose surgeons are always employed;
Where boys with soft hands
Are provided with glands,
And two-fisted girls are de-boyed.

348

There was a young girl named Maxine,
Whose vagina was wondrously clean.
With her uterus packed,
She kept safe from attack
With a dill pickle, papulous green.

349

A fair young damsel named Grace
Thought it was foolish to place
Her hand on a p***k
Once it went thick,
In case it would explode in her face.

350

An odd monk nicknamed Augustin
His rod a boy's bottom thrust in.
Then said Father Ignatius:
"Now, really! Good gracious!
Your conduct is truly disgustin'."

351

A brainy professor named Ted
Dreamed one night of a buxom co-ed.
He mussed and he bussed her
And otherwise fussed her—
But the action was all in his head.

352

A Professor who hailed from Podunk,
And was rather too frequently drunk,
Said: "Sometimes I think
That I can parse pink:
Let me see—it is pink, pank, and punk."

353

There was a young girl whose frigidity
Approached cataleptic rigidity,
Till you gave her a drink
When she quickly would sink
In a state of complaisant liquidity.

354

There was a young lady called Starkey,
Who agreed to live with a darkey.
The result of her sins
Was a nice set of quins,
Two white, two black, and one khaki.

355

There was a young fellow named Morgan,
Who possessed a remarkable organ.
The end of his dong,
Which was nine inches long,
Was tipped with the head of a gorgon.

356

There was a young man from Siam,
Who said, "I go in with a wham;
But I soon loose my starch,
Like the mad month of March,
And the lion comes out like a lamb.

357

There was a young lady of Bude,
Who walked down the street in the nude.
A bobby said: "Whattum
Magnificent bottom!"
And slapped it as hard as he could.

358

There was a young lady from Kansas,
Whose fan was as big as Bonanzas.
It was nine inches deep
And the sides were quite steep;
It had whiskers like General Carranza's.

359

There was a young fellow named Bowen,
Whose pecker kept growin' and growin'.
It grew so tremendous,
So long and so pendulous,
'Twas no good for peckin'—just showin'.

360

There was a young man of Cashmere,
Who purchased a fine Bayadere;
He diddled her toes,
Her mouth, ears, and nose,
And eventually poxed her right ear.

361

A big Catholic layman named Fox
Makes a living by playing with c***s.
  In spells of depression,
  He goes to confession
And jacks off the priest in his box.

362

A neurotic young man from Kildare
Drilled a hole in the seat of a chair.
  He ****ed it all night
  Then died of the fright
That maybe he wasn't all there.

363

There was a young lady named Hatch,
Devoted to music by Bach.
  She played with her pussy
  To "La Faun" by Debussy,
But to ragtime she just scratched her snatch.

364

A gallant young Frenchman named
Granhomme
Was attempting a girl on a tandem.
At the height of the rape
She slammed on the brake
And scattered his semen at random.

365

There was a young man from Beirut
Played a penis as one played a flute,
Till he met a sad eunuch
Who lifted his tunic
And sighed: "Sir, my instrument's mute."

366

"For the tenth time, dull Daphnis," said Chloë,
"You have told me my bosom is snowy.
You've made much verse on
Each part of my person;
Now do something—there's a good boye."

367

Growing tired of her husband's great mass
A young bride inserted some glass.
  The rod of her hubby
  Is now short and stubby,
While the wife can now piss through her ass.

368

A young lad from Kalamazoo
Who was only just learning to screw,
  Found he hadn't the knack
  And he got too far back—
In the right church, but in the wrong pew.

369

A eunuch who came from Port Said
Had a jolly good time in bed.
  Nor could any sultana
  Detect from his manner
That he used a banana instead.

370

There was a young laddie named Leitch,
Who fell asleep on a beach.
His dreams of nude women
Had his proud organ brimmin'
And squirting on all within reach.

371

A reformer who once went to Bali
To change the sartorial folly
Of the girls now admits
That a pair of fine tits
In season can seem rather jolly.

372

A lecherous parson from Pretoria
In a state of constant euphoria
Enjoyed having fun
With a whore or a nun
While chanting the Sanctus and Gloria.

373

There once was a rector of Poole
Most deservedly proud of his tool.
  With some trifling aid
  From the curate, 'tis said
He rogered the National School.

374

The swaggering hips of a jade
Raised the lust of a clerical blade.
  Hell-bent for his fun
  He went home on the run
And rogered his grandmother's maid.

375

There was a young fellow in Maine
Who courted a girl all in vain.
  She cussed when he kissed her
  So he slept with her sister
Again and again and again.

376

There was a young lady named Kate,
Who necked in the dark with her date.
  When asked how she fared,
  She said she was scared,
But otherwise doing first-rate.

377

There was a young fellow named Puttenham
Whose tool caught in doors upon shuttin' 'em.
  He said: "Well, perchance,
  It would help to wear pants
If I just could remember to button 'em."

378

A lesbian lady named Annie
Desired to appear much more manny:
  So she whittled a pud
  Of mahogany wood
And had it protrude from her fanny.

379

There was a young man from Darjeeling,
Whose dong reached up to the ceiling.
  In the electric-light socket
  He'd put it and rock it,
Crying: "God! What a wonderful feeling!"

380

An inhibited fellow from Lincoln
One night did some serious drinkin',
  Met a girl, now his wife,
  Learned the true facts of life,
And blesses the day he got stinkin'.

381

There was an old parson of Lundy
Fell asleep in his vestry one Sunday.
  He awoke with a scream:
  "What, another wet dream?
This comes from not frigging since Monday!"

382

There once was a horse named Billie
Whose dingus was really a dilly.
  It was vaginoid duply
  And labial quadruply—
In fact he was really a filly.

383

There was a young man of Toulouse,
Who had a deficient prepuce.
  But the foreskin he lacked
  He made up in his sac,
Though his balls were inclined to be loose.

384

There was a young man of Kiel,
Who liked to have a sly feel.
  On trying this ploy
  On a girl that was coy
She knackered his balls with her heel.

385

There was a young girl of Connecticut,
Who didn't care much about etiquette.
  Whenever she was able
  She'd piss on the table,
Then mop up her **** with her petticoat.

386

There was a young lady of Natchez,
Who claimed to be born with two swatches.
  She often says: "S**t!
  I would give either tit
For a man with equipment that matches."

387

There was a young fellow named Locke,
Who was born with a two-headed c**k.
  When he'd fondle the thing
  It would rise up and sing
An antiphonal chorus by Bach.

388

But whether these two ever met
Has not been recorded as yet;
Still, it would be diverting
To see him inserting
His dong while they sang a duet.

389

There was an old maid named Rice
Who was afraid of little grey mice;
Till one crept up her ****
And she said with a grunt:
"Superb! A feeling beyond price!"

390

There was a young man of Natal,
Who was ****ing a Hottentot gal.
Said she: "You're a sluggard!"
Said he: "You be buggered!
I like to **** slow, and I shall."

391

There was a young girl from Penzance,
Who decided to take just one chance.
  So she let herself go
  In the lap of her beau—
And now all her sisters are aunts.

392

A notorious whore named Miss Hearst
In the weakness of men is well versed.
  Reads a sign o'er the head
  Of her well-rumpled bed:
THE CUSTOMER ALWAYS COMES
FIRST.

393

There was an old man of Tralee,
Who was bothered to death by a flea;
  So he put out the light, saying:
  "Now he can't bite,
For he'll never be able to see."

394

There once was a gangster named Brown,
The wiliest mobster in town.
He was caught by the G-men
Shooting his semen
Where the cops would all slip and fall down.

395

To an ancient divine of Tyrone
Was the art of rebushing ****s known.
In each **** he would ram
A fine prime raw ham
And then deftly extract the white bone.

396

There was a young girl named O'Haire.
Whose body was covered with hair.
It was really quite fun
To probe with one's gun
Because her fanny might be anywhere.

397

There was a young Scot in Madrid,
Who got fifty-five ****s for a quid.
When folk asked: "Are you faint?"
He replied: "No, I ain't.
But I don't feel as good as I did."

398

There was a young chap of Moyence,
Who ****ed his own ass in defiance
Not only of custom
And morals (dad bust 'im!)
But most of the known laws of science.

399

There was a young lady named Sutton
Who said, as she carved up the mutton:
"My father preferred
The last sheep in the herd—
This is one of his children I'm cuttin'."

400

There was a young lady of Mott,
Who inserted a fly up her t**t,
  And pretended the buzz
  Was not what it was,
But something she knew it was not.

401

Randy de Coverley Fletcher
Was reputed an infamous lecher:
  When he'd take on a whore
  She'd need a rebore,
And they'd carry him out on a stretcher.

402

There was a young man of Peru,
Who had nothing whatever to do.
  So he flew to the garret
  And buggered the parrot,
And sent the result to the zoo.

403

There was a young girl of Gibraltar,
Who was raped as she knelt at the altar.
  It really seems odd
  That a virtuous God
Should answer her prayers and assault her.

404

There was an old whore named McGhee,
Who was just the right sort for a spree.
  She said: "For a ****
  I charge half a buck,
And I throw in my asshole for free."

405

There was a young fellow named Rule,
Who went to a library school.
  As he read the index
  His thoughts turned to sex
And his blood all ran to his tool.

406

Floating idly one day through the air
A circus performer named Blair
  Tied a large lump of rock
  To the end of his c**k
And shattered a balcony chair.

407

Oh that supple young man of Montrose,
Who tickled himself with his toes.
  His landlady said,
  As she made up his bed:
"My God! How that man blows his nose."

408

As a beauty I am not a star,
There are others more handsome by far.
  But my face, I don't mind it,
  For I am behind it—
It's the people in front get the jar.

409

There was a young lady of Troy,
Who invented a new kind of toy.
She sugared her thing
Both outside and in,
And had it licked off by a boy.

410

A cheerful old party of Lucknow
Remarked: "I should just like a **** now."
So he had one and spent
And said: "I'm content
Though by no means am I so c**t-struck now."

411

There was a young man of New York,
Whose morals were lighter than cork.
"Flamingoes," said he,
"Have no terrors for me—
The bird that I fear is the stork."

412

There once was a runt from Japan,
Who couldn't resist a nice fan.
  When asked for the reason,
  He said: "When in season,
I just **** all the ****s that I can."

413

There was a young girl so mild
She'd a fear of turning out wild.
  Always thinking of Jesus
  And venereal diseases
And the horrors of having a child.

414

There was a young man of St. Claire,
Who had an affair with a bear.
  But the surly old brute
  With a snap of her snoot
Left him nothing but balls and some hair.

415

There was a young lady of Gaza,
Who shaved her **** clean with a razor.
  The crabs in a lump
  Made tracks to her rump—
Which proceedings did greatly amaze her.

416

There was a young man of this nation,
Who didn't much like fornication.
  When asked: "Do you ****?"
  He said: "No, I suck
And quite often use masturbation."

417

There was a young person of Eltham,
Who seldom ****ed whores, but oft' felt 'em.
  In the lanes he would linger
  And play at stick finger;
'Twas on the way home that he smelt 'em.

418

There was a young fellow from Boston,
Who drove around in an Austin.
  There was room for his ass
  And a gallon of gas—
But his balls hung outside, and he lost 'em.

419

There was a young man from Calcutta,
Who was heard in his beard to mutter:
  "If her Bartholin's glands
  Don't respond to my hands,
I'm afraid I shall have to use butter."

420

A bad little girl in Madrid,
A most reprehensible kid,
  Told her Tante Louise
  That her fan smelled like cheese—
The worst of it was that it did!

421

There was a young farmer of Limerick,
Who started one day to trim a rick.
    The Fates gave a frown,
    The rick tumbled down,
And killed him—I don't know a grimmer trick.

422

A damsel, seductive and handsome,
Got wedged in a sleeping-room transom.
    When she offered much gold
    For release, she was told
That the view was worth more than the ransom.

423

Said a man of his small Morris Minor:
"For petting, it couldn't be finer;
    But for love's consummation
    A wagon called station
Would afford a playground diviner."

424

There was a young student named Jones
Who'd reduce any maiden to moans
    By his wonderful knowledge,
    Acquired in college,
Of nineteen erogenous zones.

425

There was a young man from Oswego,
Who fell in love with a Dago.
    He dreamt that this Venus
    Was pulling his penis
And woke up all covered with sago.

426

There once was a fellow named Bench,
Whose tool was a sturdy gut-wrench.
    With this vibrant device
    He could reach in a trice
The innermost parts of a wench.

427

There was an old person of Sark,
Who buggered a pig in the dark.
The Swine, in surprise,
Murmured: "God blast your eyes!
Do you take me for Boulton or Park?"

428

There was a young man from King's Cross,
Who amused himself frigging a horse,
Then licking the spend
As it dripped from the end,
Saying: "It tastes just like anchovy sauce."

429

There was a young lady of fashion
Who had oodles and oodles of passion.
She laughed as she said:
"Come jump into bed—
Here's one thing that Nelson can't ration."

430

There was a young fellow named Ignatius,
Who lived in a garret quite spacious.
When he went to his Aunties
He always wore panties,
But alone in the garret—good gracious!

431

I once knew a harlot named Lou,
And a versatile tart she was too.
After ten years of whoredom
She would die of sheer boredom
If she married an old bastard like you!

432

The Sultan got sore at his harem
And invented a scheme for to scare 'em:
He caught him a mouse,
Which he loosed in the house—
(The confusion is called harem-scarem).

433

Miss Minnie McFinney of Butte
Fed always, and only, on fruit.
    Said she: "Let the coarse
    Eat of beef and of horse;
I'm a peach, and that's all there is to it."

434

There was a young woman named Bright,
Whose speed was much faster than light;
    She set out one day
    In a relative way,
And returned on the previous night.

435

Mary Jane goes to bed at eleven,
Committing her welfare to Heaven:
    Her face is so pure,
    She's so good and demure—
But then, she has turned forty-seven.

436

There is a young man from the West,
Who loves a young lady with zest.
  So hard has he pressed her
  To make her say: "Yes, sir,"
That he has to keep changing his vest.

437

There was a young fellow named Doyle,
Who wrapped up his wife in tin foil.
  "For," said he, "she's so sweet,
  So neat, such a treat,
I keep having fears she will spoil."

438

A fellow named Ivor B. Ball,
Who lives in a third floor back hall:
  If you make fun of his name,
  He cries out: "Shame! Shame!
Just mind your own business, that's all!"

439

A roué who thought he was wise
Met a couple of smart-selling guys.
  They sold him a p***k
  About four inches thick—
Much to the old guy's surprise.

440

Said old Peeping Tom of Fort Lee:
"Peeping ain't what it's cracked up to be.
  I lose all my sleep,
  And I peep and I peep,
And I find 'em all peeping at me."

441

A fellow named Ted Magee,
Rolling homeward one night from a spree,
  Met a vicar who said:
  "Ah, drunk again Ted!"
"Sho'm I, Vicar," saith Magee.

442

There was a First Lady of Eden,
Who on apples was quite fond of feedin'.
  So she gave one to Adam,
  Who said: "Thank you madam,"
With which they skedaddled from Eden.

443

A certain young fellow named Beebee
Wished to wed a lady named Phoebe.
  "Phoebe," said he," I must see
  What the clerical fee be
Before Phoebe be Phoebe Beebee."

444

There was a cute girl who said: "Well,
I'm determined that I will raise Hell!"
  She concocted a scheme
  That was surely a scream—
But I promised I never would tell.

INDEX

(by key words and limerick numbers)